A GUIDE TO

REIKI

CASS & JANIE JACKSON

Published in 2002 by Caxton Editions
20 Bloomsbury Street
London WC1B 3JH
a member of the Caxton Publishing Group

© 2002 Caxton Publishing Group

Designed and produced for Caxton Editions
by Open Door Limited, Rutland, United Kingdom

Editing: Mary Morton
Setting: Jane Booth
Digital Imagery © copyright 2002 PhotoDisc Inc.

Title: A Guide to Reiki
ISBN: 1 84067 298 6

IMPORTANT NOTICE:
This book is not intended to be a substitute for medical advice or treatment.
Any person with a condition requiring medical attention should consult a qualified
medical practitioner or therapist.

A GUIDE TO
REIKI

CASS & JANIE JACKSON

CAXTON EDITIONS

CONTENTS

INTRODUCTION

The revolution in health care began when patients started to reject the drug-oriented, pills-for-everything attitude of the medical establishment. As people began to accept responsibility for their own well-being, they turned to self-help.

Below: patients have started to reject the drug-oriented, pills-for-everything attitude.

Traditional remedies, once dismissed as "old wives' tales", were found to be effective. Enthusiasm for herbal preparations led to a brisk trade in the vitamins and minerals sold in "health shops". Media interest encouraged the trend, helping to create the next development – an interest in remedial therapies rather than medicines.

These treatments differ from Western medical practice in two ways.

* *First, practitioners have an holistic approach – they treat the whole person, not merely the symptoms.*

* *Second, these therapies are natural healing arts that may have evolved over thousands of years and do not include the use of drugs.*

Typical of these methods is the ancient healing art of Reiki, which originated centuries ago in Tibet and India. Re-discovered in Japan in the middle of the 19th century, it was introduced to the West in the 1930s. A recent upsurge of interest means that Reiki is now one of the most popular and effective of all the remedial therapies available.

Below: there is now a brisk trade in vitamins and minerals.

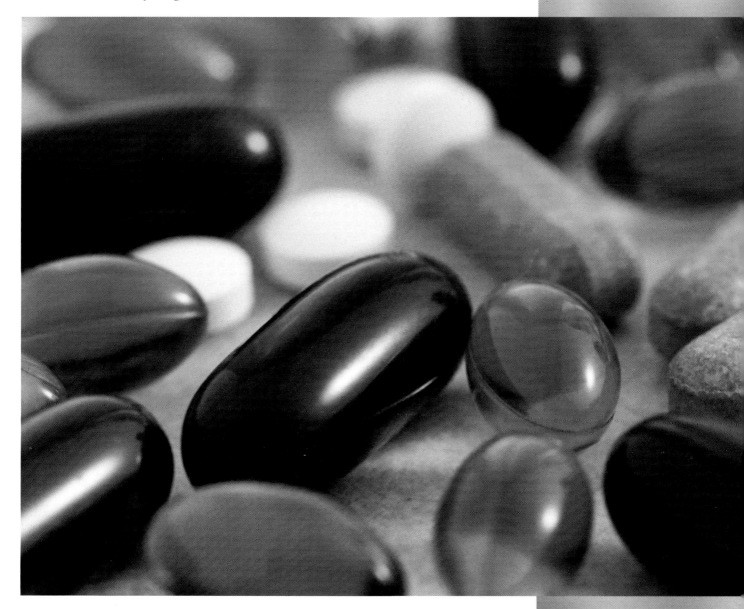

Reiki is a non-intrusive, hands-on form of natural healing which can be used to alleviate any form of disease, whether it is of the body, the mind or the spirit. Briefly, Reiki is an incredibly powerful energy that can be used in many ways.

Pronounced "ray-key", the term Reiki is a combination of two Japanese words. Rei, the first, can be translated as "universal" or "boundless". The second word, Ki, refers to the life force. Thus, the combination of the two words produces REI-KI, which means "universal life energy".

The energy known as Ki is the life force. Without it, we die. Its importance has been acknowledged in every known civilisation and it is called by many names. The Chinese refer to chi. Native Americans know it as orenda and in India it is called prana.

Reiki helps to restore and maintain the essential balance of Ki in the body.

When your life-force energy is low, you become susceptible to illness, depression and stress. All such conditions may be classed as disease, and all can be alleviated by the use of Reiki. Disease in this context refers to an imbalance of the body's energies that will lead to discomfort or distress.

Far left: when your Ki is low you become susceptible to illness, depression and stress.

Below: Reiki is a non-intrusive, hands-on form of natural healing.

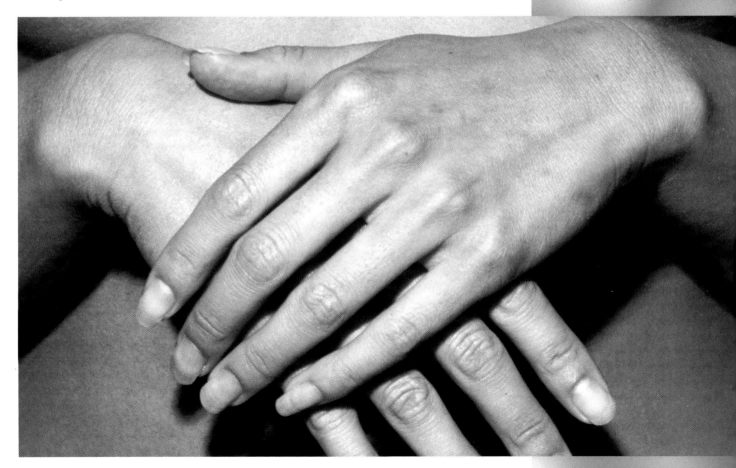

Below: a kettle cannot receive energy direct from the power point without the flex – but the flex does not provide the energy.

When you visit a Reiki practitioner, they will place their hands on your body, providing a channel through which the healing can flow. This input will restore the essential balance of the life force to your body and hence return you to good health.

Reiki practitioners do not claim to be healers. They are ordinary people who have learned to act as channels for the universal healing energies. In fact, a Reiki practitioner can be likened to a piece of flex.

The patient is comparable to an electric kettle and the universal healing energies are the power point. A kettle cannot receive energy direct from the power point without the flex. But the flex does not provide the energy – it merely conducts it.

There is no need for you to believe in Reiki – or, for that matter, in any other healing system. It will still work. After all, the kettle can boil water without having faith in the power point. Certainly Reiki is not a religion, though many people have discovered that The Five Principles (see page 28) have a profound effect on their lives.

(See also Cass's story at the end of this book.)

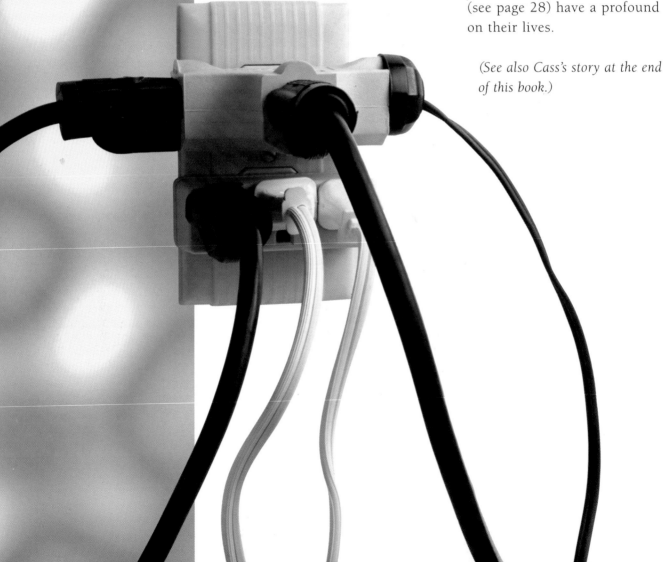

"If Jesus was able to perform miracles of healing, why can't we do the same thing?"

The speaker was a student at a Christian college in Japan. His theology teacher and principal of the college was Dr Mikao Usui. He took the young man's question seriously.

Below: if Jesus was able to perform miracles of healing, why can't we do the same thing?

"I don't know," he said. "But I will find out."

Thus, in the middle of the 19th century, began a quest that was to take many years and cover thousands of miles.

Finding nothing to help him in Japan, Dr Usui travelled to the United States, but even advanced American research facilities revealed nothing. He was equally unsuccessful in China and Tibet. When he returned to Japan, he again studied Christian texts, but still found no answer.

Above: Dr Usui saw a brilliant light in the sky.

It was while he was staying at a Zen monastery that he happened upon an ancient Buddhist manuscript. As he studied the archaic symbols, he became convinced that they contained the information he had sought for so long. The problem now was how to use the symbols to activate the healing energy.

The abbot of the monastery advised Dr Usui to go on a pilgrimage to Mount Kuri Yama, a holy mountain near Kyoto. Here he fasted and meditated for 21 days. At dawn on the final day of his retreat, he bowed his head and prayed fervently that he might be given the knowledge he was seeking.

When he opened his eyes, he saw a brilliant light in the sky. It appeared to be heading straight for him. Dr Usui watched, half-fascinated, half-afraid, as the light came closer. It struck him between the eyes.

Almost in a state of trance, he had a vision of the sacred symbols he had found in the Buddhist text. At the same time, he was told how they could be activated for healing. Thus, at dawn on top of Mount Kuri Yama, Mikao Usui was initiated into Reiki.

The story does not end there. Elated and excited, Usui began rushing down the rough paths of the mountain, anxious to share his good news. When he stubbed his toe, he scarcely noticed until it began to bleed. Then he squatted on a boulder, and folded his hands around the injury. After only a few minutes, the pain and the bleeding subsided.

He hurried on but, having fasted for 21 days, decided to stop for food. Disregarding advice to break his fast with only a light meal, he ate heartily with no ill effects.

As it happened, the young woman who served his food was crying, her face swollen and inflamed. In reply to his questions, she told him that she had severe toothache, but her father could not afford to pay for the necessary dental treatment. Dr Usui gently placed his hands on her head and within a short time the pain disappeared.

Below: Usui discovered how the sacred symbols could be activated for healing.

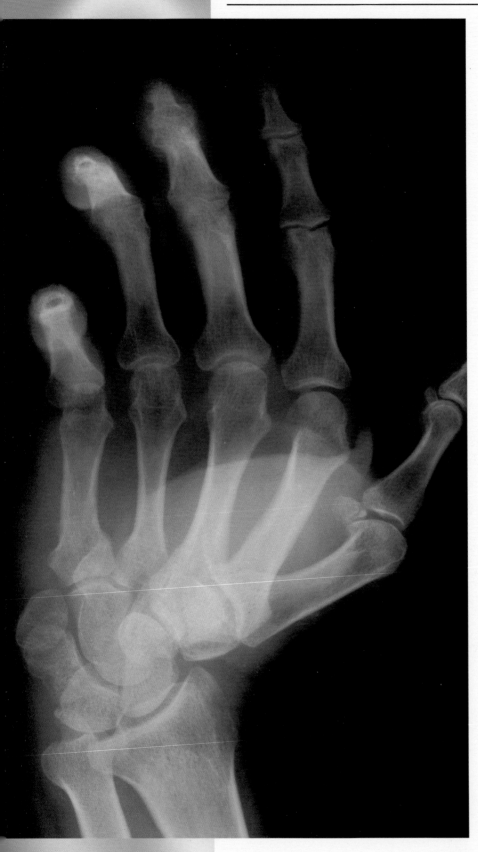

Back at the monastery, he was eager to tell the abbot about his experiences, but found that the poor man had been struck down with arthritis. Swiftly, Dr Usui applied his newly discovered knowledge. Soon the abbot was pain-free and anxious to know the secret of his cure.

Thankfully, the doctor realised that his long search for the power behind healing miracles was at an end. Now he must use his knowledge for the good of others. He abandoned his academic career and spent the next seven years in the beggars' quarter of Kyoto, healing the sick.

Then, realising that it was time to share his wisdom and spread its benefits, he began to teach Reiki to just 16 carefully selected disciples. They joined him in his healing work and, eventually, they too began to teach others

Mikao Usui died from a stroke in 1926. He was succeeded as Reiki Master by one of his disciples, Chujiro Hayashi. Gradually, the practice of Reiki began to spread throughout Japan. Clinics were opened and healing groups were formed. Eventually, in the 1930s, Reiki was introduced to the West.

Reiki is simply a means of transferring energy. As we have already explained, the practitioner acts as a channel or conduit for Ki – the universal life energy. By placing their hands on the body of the patient, they act as a conductor for that energy.

For most people, their first Reiki treatment produces a feeling of tremendous relaxation and peace. Some see colours and pictures floating behind their closed eyelids. Others see landscapes and faces. Yet some experience nothing at all and may even lie on the couch vaguely wondering when something is going to happen.

Don't worry about any reactions you may have. There are no rules, laws or expectations about this. No specific experience is mandatory. Rest assured that anything you feel is right – for you. Reiki is an intensely personal experience, which is why it is so difficult to explain.

Above: Reiki treatment produces a feeling of tremendous relaxation and peace.

Left: Dr Usui applied his newly discovered knowledge and freed an abbot of the pain he was suffering due to arthritis.

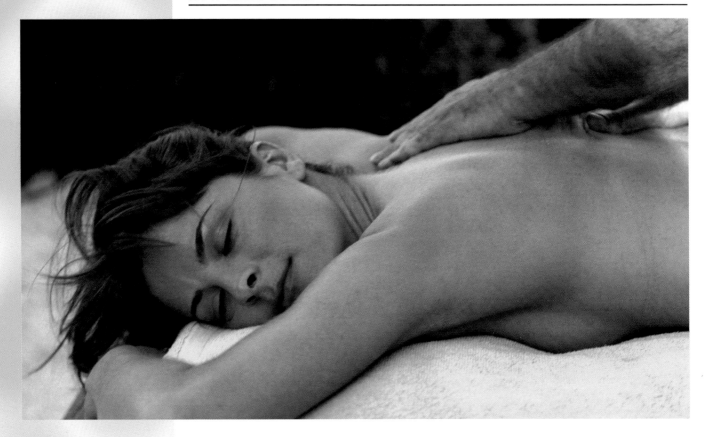

Above: it has been said that Reiki can cure anything if the patient is prepared to accept the healing.

Right: if, after four or five sessions, no improvement is seen in the condition it is best to try something else.

There is no need for you to "believe in" Reiki. On the other hand, it will be helpful if you can maintain an open attitude, welcoming the subtle life energy that is being transmitted to you. It has been said that Reiki can cure anything – but only if the patient is prepared to accept the healing.

Here again, though Reiki can usually bring about a cure, there is no guarantee that it will do so. Usually, though, symptoms will be alleviated. The patient will definitely enjoy a better quality of life and more peace of mind. This, of course, is a form of healing even if the malady itself is not cured.

Reiki is not an "instant" cure. Don't expect to hobble into the treatment room and dance out an hour later – though this can happen. After the first session, some alleviation of pain is usually experienced but instant cures are infrequent. If the ailment has recently appeared, it should respond to treatment quickly. When a problem is of long standing, more treatments will probably be needed, as the body takes time to heal itself.

There are no hard and fast laws about Reiki. Although most people find that it gives them blessed relief from pain, others may say that "it doesn't work". There are a variety of reasons why this should be. An unrecognised personality clash between practitioner and patient is one possibility. Perhaps Reiki is not suited to the particular needs of the patient, who may benefit more from another type of therapy. Sometimes – and without realising it – the patient may not wish to be healed.

If, after four or five sessions, no improvement is seen in the condition, it is best to seek help elsewhere. You may find that another Reiki practitioner will be more suited to your needs. This does not suggest that the first practitioner was lacking in any way. It is essential that there should be no praise or blame when this kind of situation arises. Calm acceptance is an important part of Reiki. Any form of stressful reaction can restrict the smooth flow of the Ki – and block the necessary healing.

YOUR FIRST EXPERIENCE OF REIKI

The preceding sections of this book have offered simple explanations about Reiki – what it is, where it originated and how it works. If you have decided to seek Reiki healing, you will want to know what to expect during your session with the practitioner. There is no need at all for you to feel nervous or apprehensive. However, we are now going to suggest a few ways in which you can prepare yourself for this new experience.

REIKI LINEAGE

As with all types of healing, it is sensible to check on the qualifications of the person who will be treating you. All qualified Reiki practitioners have what is known as a "lineage" and you would be well advised to enquire about this.

Traditionally, the Japanese revere their ancestors. Reiki practitioners take great pride in tracing their "lineage" back, through the various Masters, to Dr Usui himself. Each

Reiki Master will have received their attunements from another Master – which is how the knowledge of Reiki is passed on.

Reiki initiates each receive a copy of their lineage when they are awarded their signed certificates of competence. If the lineage is missing or cannot be proved, there is no evidence that it exists, or that the attunements are genuine and have been passed on correctly.

Below: all qualified Reiki practitioners have what is known as a "lineage".

PREPARING TO RECEIVE TREATMENT

Having satisfied yourself on these points, it is time to prepare for the treatment you are about to receive.

For a few days before your appointment, try to maintain a calm, relaxed attitude. Rest as much as possible.

Take gentle exercise. Avoid burgers and chips in favour of wholesome fresh food. Cut down on stimulants like alcohol, coffee and tea. Drink as much water as you can. And maintain a positive attitude.

On the day of your appointment, try to stay free from other demands. Allow plenty of time for your journey. You won't want to arrive at the consulting room in a state of panic, breathless and dishevelled.

Left: avoid burgers and chips in favour of wholesome fresh food.

Above: your practitioner will ask you to settle yourself on the therapy couch. You will remain fully clothed, except for removing your shoes and outdoor wear. You may close your eyes, if you wish, but this is not obligatory.

MEETING YOUR PRACTITIONER

Even if you are somewhat stressed when you arrive, you will immediately notice the calm serenity of the room in which the treatment is to take place.

The session will start with conversation. The practitioner will ask if you have any special reason for seeking treatment. If you have, do explain your problems clearly. Tell them, too, if you are receiving other medical help or if you are taking any form of medication. If, on the other hand, you are simply "trying it out", don't be afraid to say so. They will be pleased to give you a brief explanation of what Reiki does and how it works.

Next, they will ask you to settle yourself on the therapy couch. You will remain fully clothed, except for removing your shoes and outdoor wear. Try to relax, and do ensure that you are completely comfortable before treatment begins. You may close your eyes, if you wish, but this is not obligatory.

RECEIVING TREATMENT

The treatment will probably begin with the smoothing of the aura. This means that the practitioner will pass their hands through the air from your head to your toes, about eight inches above your body. At this stage, they will not touch you, but you are likely to experience a sensation of utter tranquillity.

Next comes the Reiki treatment itself. The practitioner will gently place their hands in various positions on your body. Half way through the session, you will be asked to turn over so that they can treat your back.

At the end of the treatment – which usually takes about an hour – they may again smooth the aura.

Your first Reiki treatment is complete.

Below: the practitioner will gently place their hands in various positions on your body.

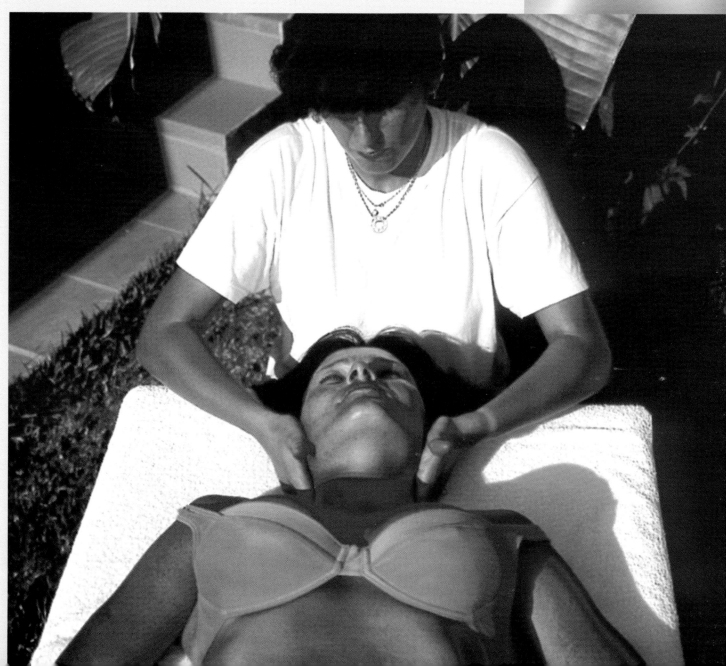

HOW WILL I FEEL?

Individual reactions to Reiki differ. The most common is to feel warmth emanating from the practitioner's hands. Others feel that cool water is rippling along their limbs. Some experience "pins and needles". Others feel nothing at all and wonder, "When is it going to start?" Yet others feel as if they are floating gently through the air, in complete security.

Reactions vary from person to person and from treatment to treatment, but the most common is a sense of peace and relaxation. For this reason, we advise you to remain on the couch for a few minutes on completion of treatment. Don't be tempted to leap up and hurry away. Breathe quietly and gently, gradually returning to the "real" world.

When you begin to stir, your practitioner will advise you to sit up slowly and to "ground" yourself, by rubbing the palms of your hands together and scuffing the soles of your feet on the floor.

Far right: within a couple of days you will be feeling the full benefit of your first experience of Reiki.

Below: reactions to Reiki differ some feel that cool water is rippling along their limbs.

AFTER TREATMENT

Be aware that, after the first treatment, you may experience what is known as a "healing crisis". This usually takes the form of a sudden cold or a slight tummy upset. It is caused by the dispersal of the energy blockages in your system. Within a couple of days, you will undoubtedly be feeling the full benefit of your first experience of Reiki.

BECOMING A REIKI PRACTITIONER

Many people who have benefited from Reiki treatment eventually decide they would like to become practitioners. Some wish to do self-healing – that is, using Reiki methods on themselves. Some have the desire to share their knowledge more widely and heal others. Anyone can take Reiki training. Age, sex, colour, and creed matter not at all.

Above: some people who have benefited from Reiki have the desire to share their knowledge more widely and heal others.

Whatever your reason for wishing to become a practitioner, you will almost certainly be surprised by the ease with which the healing power is passed to you through the hands of your Master. But there is more to Reiki training than the transmission of energy, and several aspects must be considered before you actually seek attunement.

REACHING A DECISION

* *First – why do you want to become a practitioner? Do be sure that this is not just a whim – something to give you a new interest or to impress your friends.*

* *Second – who will be your teacher? You are strongly advised to have at least one Reiki treatment from this person before you undertake training. Ensure that you have confidence in them and that you feel at ease in their company. And remember to check their credentials, as advised on page 18.*

When you have decided that this is the right path for you, ask your intended Reiki Master if they are willing to guide you through the basic principles, be your mentor and give you the necessary attunements. You will be told that there are three sets of attunements starting with the First Degree, through to the Second Degree, and finally the Reiki Master Degree. Most Reiki Masters are willing to undertake the training of students. They will first want to spend a long period of time chatting to you about your reasons for wanting to become a Reiki practitioner. Be sure to have your answers ready before you meet for your introductory talk.

If the Master feels that you are ready, they will explain to you what is involved in each of the three levels of attunement and exactly what is expected of you. Theye will also want to know if you have any questions.

Below: you will need to explain about your reasons for wanting to become a Reiki practitioner to the Reiki Master you approach for tuition.

WHAT WILL IT COST?

If you have not already discussed the question of fees, do so now. Throughout Reiki, there are varying opinions on the subject of money. Some Masters make no charge for attunements, believing that Reiki should be free for all to practise. Others may suggest astronomical fees.

There are several reasons for this. During his early healing work, Dr Usui came to realise that people rarely valued anything that was given freely. As a result, Reiki Masters introduced a system of appren-ticeships, where the student acted as an unpaid servant in return for receiving the attunements. Later, as this system became outmoded, the student was expected to pay the Reiki Master a sum of money comparable to the cost of their apprenticeship. This eventually became a fixed fee, decided upon by the Reiki Union of Masters, and was set at $10,000. – or £7,000

Nowadays, you will be quoted a range of fees, largely dependent upon how long your Master spends in coaching you. Some take several days for each attunement. Others will initiate you into Levels 1 and 2 over a weekend. Yet others offer the two attunements in one day.

Don't rush into any decision. It's tempting to go for the quickest, cheapest course you can find. Our personal view, based on experience, is that you get what you pay for. Some Masters – particularly those who charge higher fees – claim that the money will be forthcoming if you are destined to become a practitioner. This belief, perhaps, is based on the Zen koan that "When the pupil is ready, the Master appears".

More prosaically, we advise you to shop around. Decide how much you can afford to pay. Check on the Masters offering attunements within your financial limits. If you find one whose approach particularly appeals to you, it will be worthwhile to wait until you have saved the money needed. Try not to be overly concerned about the financial aspect. In our experience it is usually true that the money becomes available when the time is right

Far right: the money becomes available when the time is right.

Below: a fixed fee, decided upon by the Reiki Union of Masters, was set at $10,000 – or £7,000.

THE FIVE PRINCIPLES

One of the first lessons you will learn concerns the Five Principles of Reiki. These form an integral part of Dr. Usui's teachings. One tradition holds that they were revealed to him during his meditation on Mount Kuri Yama. Another belief is that he created them during the time that he worked in the beggars' quarter in Kyoto. Whatever the truth, these are the Reiki "laws" he laid down. Study them carefully. If you are to become a Reiki practitioner, it is important that you feel able to live by them.

Below: just for today, I will not worry.
Just for today, I will not get angry.

THE FIVE PRINCIPLES OF REIKI

* *Just for today, I will not worry.*

* *Just for today, I will not get angry.*

* *Just for today, I will honour and respect all living things.*

* *Just for today, I will earn my living honestly.*

* *Just for today, I will give thanks for my many blessings.*

These principles encapsulate Dr Usui's conviction that we all need to accept responsibility for our own actions. The actual wording has varied over the years and from Master to Master. However, the meaning behind each one is as applicable today as it was when Reiki originated. It is interesting, too, to note the use of the "one day at a time" attitude currently used in the "twelve step" programmes recommended by organisations such as Alcoholics Anonymous etc. These are based on the theory that only NOW exists. The past is gone. The future is yet to come. There is only today. Live each day as though it is your last.

ATTUNEMENTS

We have already explained that you will be "attuned" to Reiki, rather than taught it. So what do we mean by the word "attunement"? The dictionary definition is "to bring into harmony". This is exactly what happens when a student is connected to the Reiki healing energy.

There are three degrees of Reiki, known simply as Levels 1, 2 and 3. As already explained, the time taken for the various attunements varies. Usually, each occupies two days. Some Masters offer initiations into Levels 1 and 2 together at one weekend course, followed by attunement as a Master shortly after. In effect, this means that it is possible to become a Reiki Master within a matter of weeks. Undoubtedly, this accelerated system suits some people. However, any Reiki attunement increases the student's vibratory rate and some find the compressed teaching system too much to cope with. Indeed, some Reiki Masters recommend leaving one to three years between attunements.

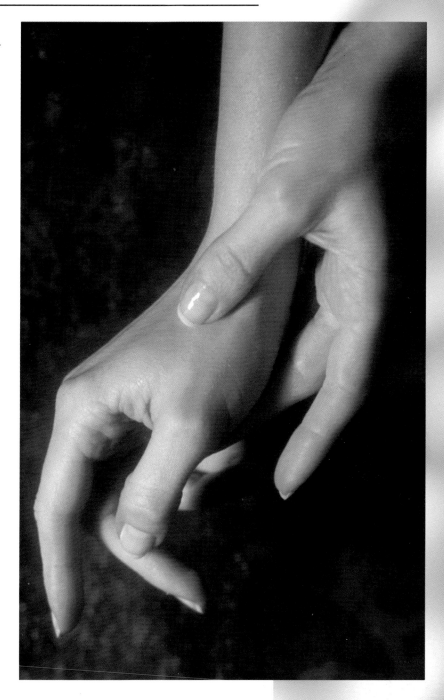

Above: Reiki attunement increases the student's vibratory rate.

Above: Masters are prepared to conduct group initiations which can involve 10 people or more.

Initiation into each level of Reiki requires a specific ceremony or ritual. As with all other aspects of the system, these vary from Master to Master. Usually, the attunement concerns only two people – the student and the Master. However, some Masters are prepared to conduct group initiations involving 10 people or more. This can have certain advantages in that members of the group are able to swap experiences and discuss their feelings with other group members. Traditionally, though, attunement is considered to be such a personal event that only the pupil and the Master should be present.

LEVEL 1

This, the first Reiki level, is the basic course and effectively "switches on" the healing power. The process is simple, but can be deeply moving for the student.

If you are new to energy work and/or healing, you should give careful consideration to the timing most likely to suit your temperament. Discuss this with your Master and accept their advice. Calmness and composure are basic tenets of Reiki at any level, and nothing will be gained from rushing the whole procedure.

Dr Usui himself found his initiation to all three Reiki levels so overwhelming that he lost consciousness. Subsequently, he developed methods of imparting his teachings gradually. Even today, in our "instant" society, this is the more usual form of Reiki attunement.

At the beginning of the attunement ritual, you will be invited to sit comfortably in a straight-back chair. Initially, you will be asked to place your palms together in the "praying" position. This will change at various stages of the ceremony, but the Master will quietly guide you to adopt the correct posture.

Left: you will be asked to place your palms together in the "praying" position.

Throughout the ritual, the Master acts as a channel for the energy they are transmitting to the student. They begin by standing behind you and drawing certain symbols in the air. This process is repeated in front of you, with the Master silently performing the initiation rituals. When they have completed these, they will resume their position behind your chair. Beginning with the crown chakra, at the top of your head, they will pass their hands over your body, incorporating and activating each of the chakras. The ceremony ends when you are "grounded" via the root chakra.

Below: the ceremony is usually followed by a meditation.

This means that you are now connected with the Reiki energy and that you will remain so for the rest of your life.

The ceremony is usually followed by a meditation, after which the Master will instruct you on Reiki healing methods. This is when you will learn the correct hand positions required for healing yourself and other people. The diagrams you will be given may seem complex at first sight, but you will swiftly be able to commit them to memory.

Most Masters advise students to give themselves a Reiki treatment every day for 21 days – an echo here of Dr Usui's pilgrimage to Mount Kuri Yama. You should also give healing to other people as often as possible. All this facilitates the flow of the Reiki energy throughout the chakras. As the days pass, you will find your awareness of this energy will increase. You will almost certainly notice, too, that your own health will improve.

REIKI GROUPS

With the increasing popularity of this therapy, Reiki groups have been formed in most areas and these can be of great value to the newly initiated. It is worth making enquiries about such groups in your locality – health stores can often guide you in the right direction.

THE NEXT STEP

Not everyone who takes Level 1 Reiki will want to continue on to Level 2. Indeed, if your main concern is to treat yourself, family and friends, Level 1 level will be adequate for your needs. Be aware, though, that this does not qualify you to set up as a Reiki practitioner and to charge for healing. Whatever your aims may be, you should consider carefully what Level 2 involves.

When you took your first attunement, the changes you experienced were mainly physical – a type of cleansing process. The second attunement deals with your emotional, mental and spiritual healing and may well be the catalyst for a number of unexpected reactions. These are likely to concern half-forgotten factors from the past that need to be dealt with. Old quarrels, failures, mistakes and negative attitudes may resurface, requiring attention. This process may take several months and can be painful, but it is a vital part of healing.

Below: old quarrels, failures, mistakes and negative attitudes may resurface.

Above: level 2 involves a commitment to your own self-development and to healing others.

Traditionally, students are advised to allow at least three months between attunements for Levels 1 and 2. This waiting period enables you to adjust to the influx of energy and the re-balancing taking place as a result of the first initiation.

The decision to proceed to Level 2 should be made only if you wish to become more deeply involved in Reiki. Understand that this will involve a commitment to your own self-development and to healing others. Reiki is not a discipline that can be used merely when you happen to think of it. It should become an integral part of your self and your life.

You will not be eligible for Level 2 attunement until you have completed Level 1 and have had some experience of healing others. This, at any rate, is the traditional view but we are all individuals and some people may find the accelerated path mentioned earlier more to their liking.

Left: three of the sacred Reiki symbols.

highly secret. The student was expected to memorise them immediately and any drawings were destroyed before the end of the ritual. In recent years, however, the symbols have been widely published and they are also available on the Internet. Even so, they are still regarded as sacred and should never be displayed or discussed with outsiders.

When the meaning of each symbol has been explained to you, you will probably be invited to express your own ideas about it. Don't be shy about this. Your perceptions are valuable and may well enhance those of other people, including your Master.

You are now ready to go – to heal yourself and others.

LEVEL 2

The physical pattern for Level 2 attunement is similar to that for Level 1. You will again be seated and the Master will work around you. This time, though, because you have already been attuned to Reiki energy, you will be more aware of what is happening.

At the start of this ceremony, you will be taught three of the Reiki symbols. At one time, these were regarded as

DISTANT HEALING

After you have learned the symbols – or at least made a start on memorising them – they will be empowered through your attunement. This will enable you to undertake Distant Healing – that is, healing a person who is not physically present – and you will be instructed how to do this.

As with Level 1, this attunement ceremony will usually conclude with a meditation.

This time, though, you may be asked to go away and fulfil certain obligations before your Master will give you your Level 2 certificate of competence. These requirements vary from Master to Master, but may involve something like giving and receiving three full hands-on treatments, using Second Degree symbols, and also undertaking a full Distant Healing every day for 30 days.

Below: Distant Healing is, healing a person who is not physically present – and you will be instructed how to do this.

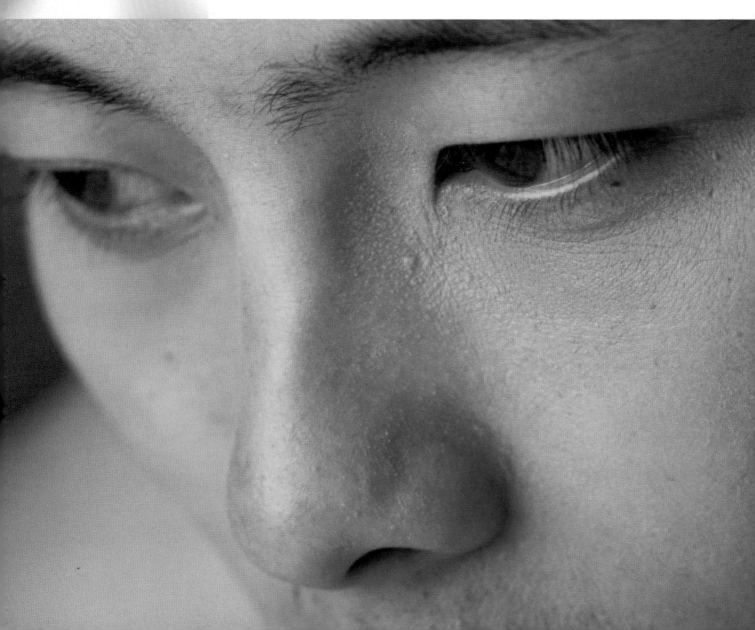

As you have now discovered, Reiki is completely different from all other methods of healing. Unlike other therapies, it is not taught. Instead, the student is "attuned" to Reiki power. And this enables you to act as a channel or pipeline to pass the healing energy on to others.

Your Master will have explained that the more you use this Reiki energy, the stronger it will become. You will soon become aware of this and – naturally – will feel some excitement as a result. This is when you need to remember the importance of a calm, deliberate approach.

One way to do this is to develop what can only be described as an holistic lifestyle. The old admonition "Physician, heal thyself" expresses perfectly the vital need for you, the healing channel, to be at peace with yourself before you attempt to deal with the problems of others.

Below: "Physician, heal thyself" expresses perfectly the vital need for you, the healing channel, to be at peace with yourself before you attempt to deal with the problems of others.

THE HOLISTIC APPROACH

Most people understand that the term "holistic" encompasses every aspect of our being – body, mind and spirit. Now that you have taken Reiki training, you need to ensure that all three aspects of the essential YOU are balanced and healthy.

✱ Maintain a healthy body by eating sensibly, taking sufficient exercise, and ensuring that you get adequate rest. There is no such thing as a Reiki diet, but many practitioners find that a quasi-vegetarian regime works well. Avoid red meat and fatty foods. Eat plenty of fresh fruit and vegetables. Drink lots of water.

Below: eat plenty of fresh fruit and vegetables as part of your holistic lifestyle.

✱ So far as exercise is concerned, walking and swimming are ideal. Yoga, in addition to keeping your body supple, will help you to maintain a calm reflective attitude of mind.

✱ Rest does not necessarily equate with sleep and is very much a matter of personal preference. If you know that you need eight hours' sound sleep every night – that's fine. You may find, though, that an afternoon nap and fewer hours of nocturnal slumber will suit you better. Listen to your body. It will guide you to a regime that suits its needs. Your aim is to greet each new day with a clear mind and an optimistic outlook.

* Mental (and emotional) health depends completely on your personal attitude to life. Remember that we all create our own reality. Adopt an upbeat, positive approach to every situation you encounter. As a result, you will be happy – and happiness is our birthright.

* Spiritual well-being is essential if you are to gain the most possible benefit from Reiki and to pass that on to other people. It is difficult to define spiritual health. Probably the most accurate definition is "inner peace". How you obtain and maintain this much desired state is for you to decide. For some people, prayer is the answer. Others turn to meditation. Try meditating on one of the Reiki symbols. Reading spiritual books or listening to inspirational tapes can help, too. You may find your own inner peace by walking in woods or on the seashore, by gardening, by spending time with loving friends – even by cooking, painting or drawing. Look for your own spiritual path and you will find it.

Above: you may find inner peace by walking in woods or on the seashore.

Below: one way to prepare for Reiki treatment is by the use of prayer.

PRAYERS AND INVOCATIONS

Another way in which you can prepare yourself for giving or receiving Reiki treatment is by the use of prayer and/or invocations. These, recited before the healing session begins, have the effect of calming the mind and focusing it on what you are about to do. Several well-known prayers are suitable for use in this way. One is the Prayer of St Francis of Assisi.

*Lord, make me a channel of
your peace.
Where there is hatred, let me sow love.
Where there is injury, pardon.
Where there is doubt, faith.
Where there is darkness, light.
Where there is despair, hope
And where there is sadness, joy.
Divine Master, grant that I may not so
much seek to be consoled
as to console.
To be understood as to understand
To be loved as to love.
For it is in giving that we receive,
It is in pardoning that we are pardoned,
And in dying that we are born to
eternal life.*

The Great Invocation, channelled many years ago by Alice Bailey and still used by the Lucis Trust, is also popular.

From the point of Light within the Mind of God
Let light stream forth into the minds of men.
Let Light descend on Earth.

From the point of Love within the Heart of God
Let love stream forth into the hearts of men.
May Christ return to Earth.

From the centre where the Will of God is known
Let purpose guide the little wills of men.
Thy purpose which the Masters know and serve.

From the centre which we call the race of men
Let the Plan of Love and Light work out,
And may it seal the door where evil dwells.

Let Light and Love and Power restore the Plan on Earth.

If you are not a Christian, you may prefer to find something more in line with your own beliefs. Why not compose your own invocation? Use simple, ordinary words and be sure that they express your own intentions when dealing with Reiki. Just a few lines, written from the heart, will be sufficient. And the more often you use them, the more meaningful they will become.

Below: why not compose your own invocation? Use simple, ordinary words.

SELF-HEALING

The first form of Reiki treatment you will learn will be self-healing. It is also the most important. Daily self-healing is not meant only for newcomers to Reiki. It is a discipline with which you should always begin your day. Making this a habit will not only ensure the maintenance of your own good health and balanced energies, it will also guarantee that the healing energy will be more easily channelled to the people you treat. You should become accustomed to giving yourself healing, before attempting to help others. Self-healing is the foundation for all the work you undertake, now and in the future.

Below: no matter how many tasks await your attention, the self-healing session will enable you to attend to them efficiently and easily.

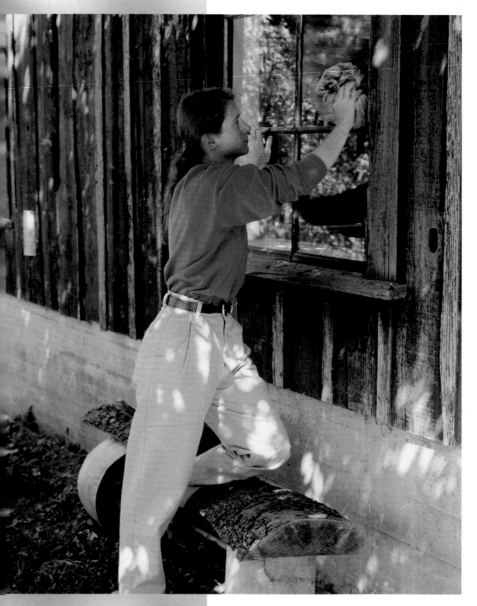

Ideally, as we have said, you should start the day with self-healing. You will find that if you wish you could conduct the whole session before you get out of bed. Nothing else that you need to do can be more important. No matter how many tasks await your attention, the self-healing session will enable you to attend to them efficiently and easily.

First, though, you need to learn the necessary hand positions. Try to commit them to memory before you start practising Reiki. The easiest way to learn the positions is to prop the instructions up in front of you while you do them. This may be sufficient for you. Perhaps you can make a rough sketch of each position. Or you could copy out the instructions for the placing of your hands. Committing instructions to paper is considered a good way to memorise anything. As with every aspect of Reiki, choose the method you prefer.

HAND POSITIONS FOR SELF-HEALING

Remember to keep your fingers together, not splayed out, and keep the thumbs close to the fingers. Always begin your healing at the top of the head and work down the body to the feet.

Hold each position for about two minutes. This means that the entire session will occupy about half an hour. If you really cannot spare that long, reduce the time to suit your needs. Remember – "half a loaf is better than none" – and 10 minutes of Reiki is to be preferred to none at all.

Before you begin the self-treatment, you should remove any metal objects you may be wearing, particularly rings or a watch.

1 Start by gently placing your hands over your eyes, the fingers pointing upwards.

NB: *Position 5 should be used only during self-healing, not when treating others.*

2 Move your hands to the side, placing your thumbs below your ears and your palms on your cheeks.

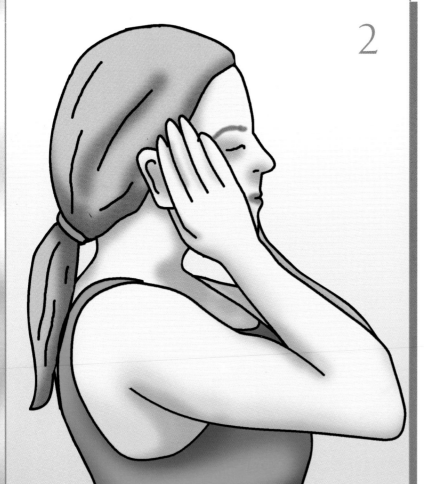

3 Position your palms at the back of your head, either side by side or one above the other.

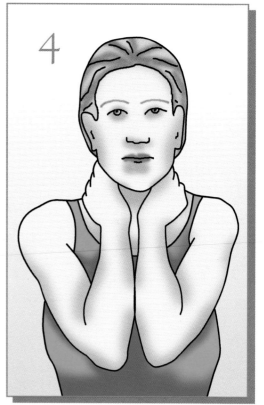

4 Place your hands over your throat. If this feels uncomfortable, you may put your hands over your collarbone instead.

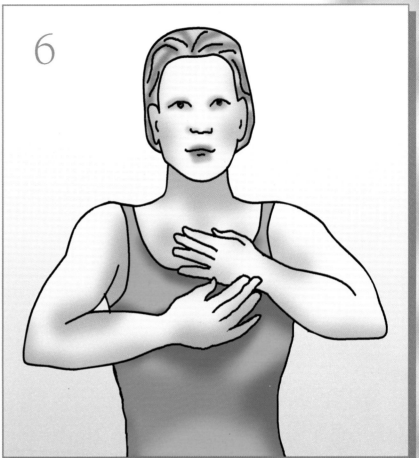

6 Put your hands over the breastbone or heart.

5 Your hands should be placed over your lower ribs, with fingertips touching.

NB As with Position 5, Position 9 should be used only during self-healing, not when treating others.

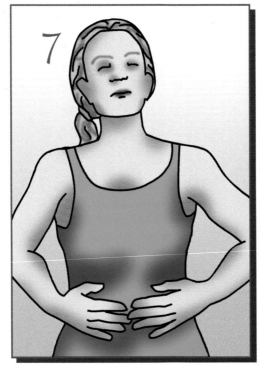

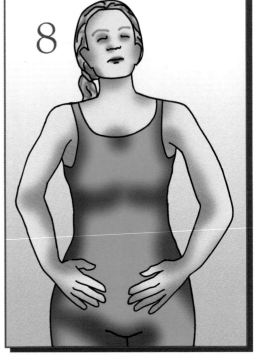

7 Now move your hands so that one is on each side of your navel, again with fingers facing.

8 Lower the hands so that they cover the pelvic bones.

NB: *Position 9 should be used only during self-healing, not when treating others.*

9 Put your hands over pubic area.

This completes the first part of the self-healing process. You will realise that basically the hands move gently down the body from one area to another. The next step is to conclude your self-treatment by dealing with the lower torso.

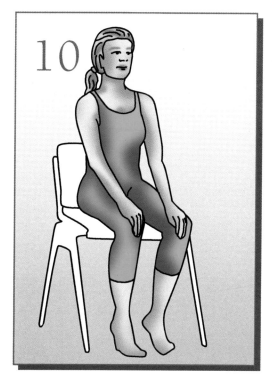

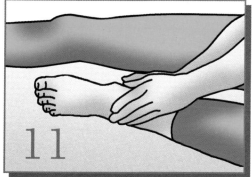

11 Move your hands to your ankles – one at a time, if this is more comfortable for you. You may prefer to cross your legs to achieve this position.

10 Place your hands over your knees, fingers pointing down.

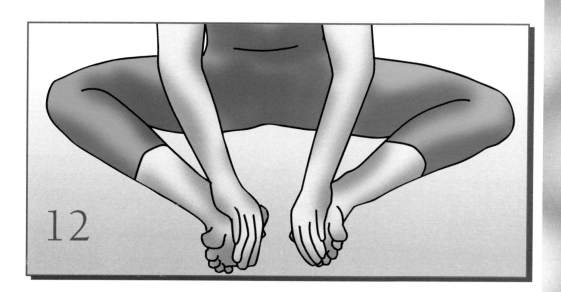

12 Finally, place your palms on the soles of your feet.

This concludes your self-healing for the power points on the front of your body. Now it is time to move to the back.

13 Place one hand on the top of your head (the crown) and the other at the back, just above the nape of your neck.

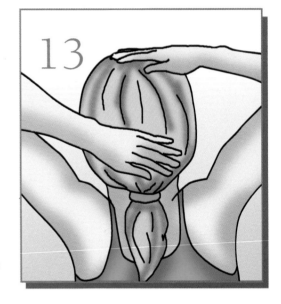

14 Next, put your hands on the back of your neck and, if you can, over the shoulder muscles, fingers pointing down.

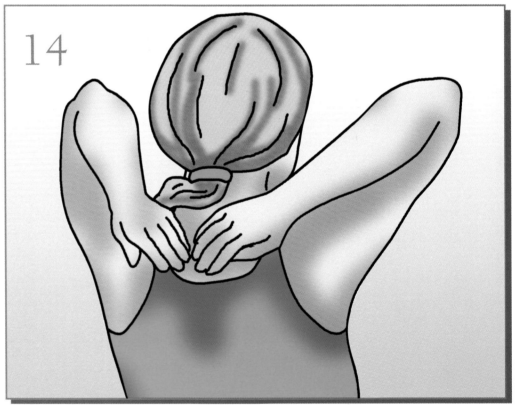

15 Bring the hands to the middle of the waist.

Position 15 brings you to the end of your self-healing session.

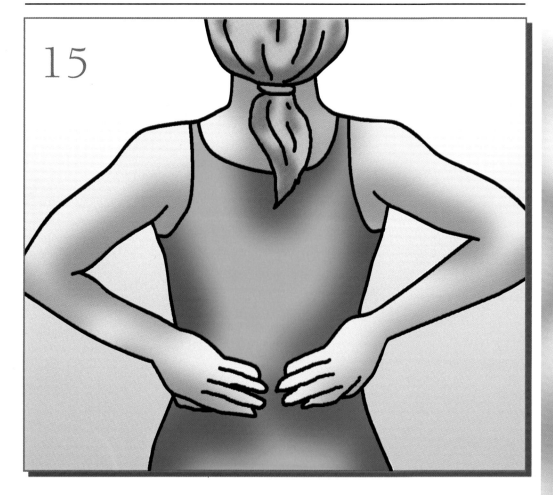

15

At first reading, these instructions may seem complicated and time-consuming. Do persevere. You will swiftly find that you become accustomed to the routine, and the benefit you gain from regularly starting your day in this way will be well worth the time involved.

When you have completed your self-healing session, rest quietly for a few minutes. Don't be tempted to jump up and rush about your chores. Remember, too, to ground yourself by rubbing your palms together and scuffing the soles of your feet on the floor. You may like to sip a glass of water before "coming back to earth".

Above: some people may find certain healing positions uncomfortable or even painful. if this applies to you, simply move on to the next position.

Some people may find certain self-healing positions uncomfortable or even painful. If this applies to you, simply move on to the next position. The healing power being channelled through your hands will find its way to the place where it is needed.

You may find yourself "guided" to place your hands elsewhere than in one of the traditional positions. Follow your intuition. There is no "right" or "wrong" way to give Reiki.

At your Level 2 attunement you will be introduced to three of the sacred Reiki symbols. This information greatly enhances the flow of energy and enables you to reduce the time spent on each hand position from five minutes to three, or even less.

Below: you will be introduced to three of the sacred Reiki symbols at Level 2.

Below: some practitioners refer to the three symbols as "the golden keys".

During this attunement you will study the symbols and copy them on to paper. Don't worry if it takes you some time to become really familiar with them. For most people, the symbolism concept is completely new and outside anything they have previously experienced. If you have problems in committing these signs to memory, keep calm. When the time is right for you to use the Reiki symbols, you will find that you are able to do so without effort. Your Reiki attunements have already placed the symbols in your subconscious. They will surface when needed.

Some practitioners refer to the three symbols as "the golden keys", because they figuratively open doors to new aspects of healing. Let's now take a further look at these three symbols, consider what they mean and how you can use them.

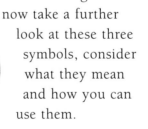

The first symbol enables the practitioner to give what is known as Distant Healing – that is, you can give a Reiki treatment to somebody who is not physically present.

The name of the symbol is **Hon Sha Ze Sho Nen**, pronounced as Hone Shah Zay Show Nen. It is written in Japanese calligraphy and translates as "The Buddha in me acknowledges the Buddha in you".

The colour related to this symbol is white on a cobalt background, and the element is air.

Left: Sei He Ki, "I hold the key to peace" is related to the colour blue and the element is water.

The second symbol is known as the Emotional and Mental Symbol. It enables the practitioner to relax the patient and to direct energy to deal with mental/emotional problems. The name of the symbol is **Sei He Ki**, pronounced Say Hay Key. This symbol is written in Sanskrit and translates as "I hold the key to peace".

The colour related to this symbol is blue and the element is water.

The third symbol is the Power Symbol, the only one that may be drawn in two ways – clockwise and anti-clockwise. Clockwise use brings energy into you, the practitioner. The anti-clockwise direction sends energy to others. The name of the symbol is **Cho-Ku-Rei** and it is pronounced Chock Yoo Ray. This means "I call on Universal Energy". This symbol is sometimes referred to as "the switch" because it is used to increase or "switch on" Reiki power.

The colour related to this symbol is red and the element is fire.

USING THE SACRED SYMBOLS

THE FIRST SYMBOL – DISTANT HEALING

As its name implies, this symbol is used to send Reiki over a distance. The actual distance involved doesn't matter. You can give healing to a loved one on the other side of the world or to a neighbour in the house next door.

Hon-Sha-Ze-Sho-Nen is also used to pass Reiki energy to anyone who is seriously ill or dying and therefore unable to accept the hand positions on his/her body. In these circumstances, the practitioner simply stands at a distance from the bed and "beams" the Reiki energy towards the sick person.

It is generally accepted that Reiki should not be sent to anyone without their consent. However, there can be dozens of situations in which it is impossible to obtain this permission, and we feel that common sense should prevail. It would seem quite ridiculous to deny the blessing of healing to sufferers merely because they are too ill to be able to agree. As with all aspects of Reiki – follow your intuition. **Intent** is of primary importance. Provided you are acting with love, go ahead.

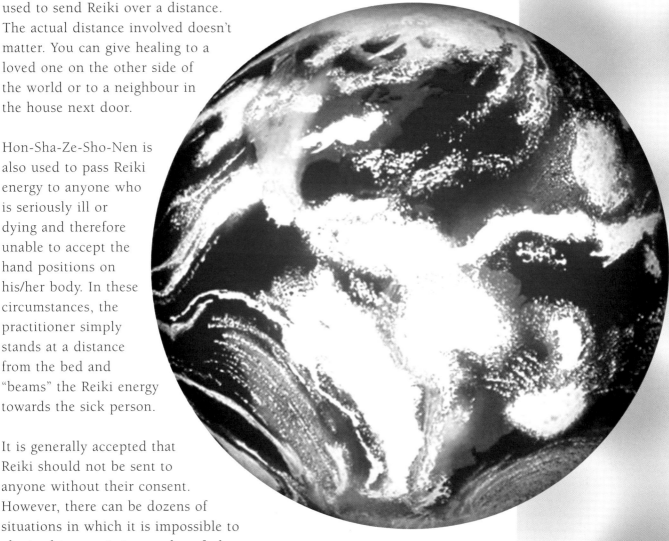

Below: you can give healing to a loved one on the other side of the world.

If it is possible to obtain consent to give Distant Healing, we suggest you set up a "meeting time". That is, tell the patient that you will be sending Reiki healing at a certain time each day and invite him/her to focus on receiving it.

Below: obtain a photograph or portrait of the person to be healed. Make the Distant Healing symbol over it.

HOW TO GIVE DISTANT HEALING

If you normally begin a Reiki session with a mantra or invocation, use it now. Then proceed with the treatment as follows.

1 Wherever possible, obtain a photograph or portrait of the person to be healed. Make the Distant Healing symbol over it and repeat the person's name. Then position the photograph in front of you.

2 Draw the symbol in the air three times. You may also care to repeat its meaning, mentally or aloud. "The Buddha in me acknowledges the Buddha in you."

3 Beam healing energy towards the person you are treating. You may also, if you wish, visualise the patient surrounded by golden light.

4 For the practitioner, Distant Healing is much more demanding than hands-on treatment. You are advised to set a time limit of 20 minutes on any one such session. At the end of that time, draw the symbol in the air as a signal that the session is closed.

There is no reason for not repeating the 20-minute treatment on the same day, but do ensure that you are completely rested and relaxed before you start. If you are worried or weary, you will effectively block the healing energy and will not help your patient or yourself.

THE SECOND SYMBOL – EMOTIONAL/MENTAL HEALING

The second symbol is often used to calm an anxious patient before starting the Reiki session. Some practitioners use it for 10 minutes at the beginning of a hands-on treatment (or five minutes in the case of Distant Healing).

Study this symbol, and you will notice that it is clearly divided into left and right, representing both masculine and feminine aspects. By harmonising the left and right sides of the brain, it connects our physical, mental and emotional bodies, providing the balanced energy we all need.

This symbol is particularly helpful in cases of addiction and depression. Its harmonising qualities clarify the problems causing the condition. This, in turn, releases emotional or mental blocks.

The Sei-He-Ki energy can be invoked for healing any form of emotional or mental distress.

Below: Sei He Ki is particularly helpful in cases of addiction and depression.

Below: Cho-Ku-Rei is the switch needed to let the power flow.

THE THIRD SYMBOL – POWER

As previously explained, the Power Symbol is the one that "switches on" and increases the flow of energy. Many practitioners notice that when they draw Cho-Ku-Rei during a healing session, their bodies are suffused by a flush of warmth.

This symbol is in some ways the most potent of those given at the Level 2 attunement. Primarily, it dramatically increases Reiki energy. It also offers protection and, used at the end of a healing session, "seals in" the energy transmitted to the patient.

If we use our former example of an electric kettle, we can recognise Cho-Ku-Rei as the switch needed to let the power flow.

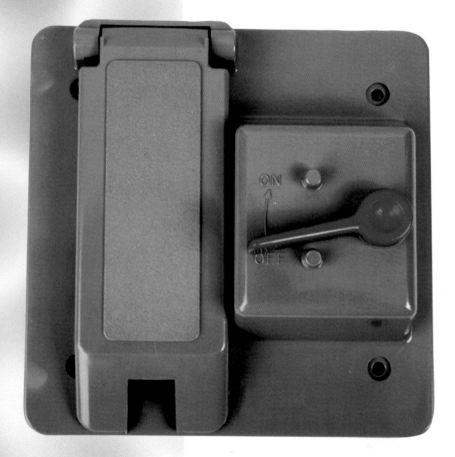

Becoming a Reiki Master is not a matter to be taken lightly. Indeed, you may well find that the decision is not entirely up to you. The Master who gave you your previous attunements may consider that you are not yet ready to undertake the responsibility of this third degree. Some Masters are unwilling to give the necessary further attunements until they are confident that the student is prepared to devote a considerable part of their life to Reiki.

That being so, please consider the matter carefully before deciding to go ahead. Perhaps your life is too busy for you to feel sure that you will be able to give time to new responsibilities. Don't feel that you "ought to" make the time. We all need to enjoy socialising and relaxation, and any sense of obligation will militate against your success as a Reiki practitioner.

WHY DO YOU WANT TO BECOME A MASTER?

At this stage, it is essential that you should ask yourself why you want to become a Reiki Master. Consider the following questions.

* *Are you sure that you are not merely seeking the "feel good" factor – the status – that becoming a Reiki Master will give you?*

* *Do you feel a genuine desire to increase your involvement with Reiki?*

* *Do you honestly have the time to do this?*

* *Do you feel within yourself a strong connection to Reiki?*

Below: we all need to enjoy socialising and relaxation.

Below: the final sacred symbol, the Master symbol, Dai-Ko-Mio.

The final question may seem strange. Think about it. If you **are** connected, you will know, beyond all possible doubt, that you too must attain Mastery. Until you feel this conviction, our advice is to practise and enjoy Reiki at the level you have already achieved. Relax into Reiki. You will be surprised at how much it will change your attitude to life and to other people.

It often happens that the decision to train as a Master arrives quietly and gently, just when the student has almost ceased to consider this step. Then what?

Trust in that inner voice and in Reiki. As soon as you are absolutely sure of what you wish to do, find a Master who is willing to give the final attunements. This may or may not be the same person who attuned you to previous levels. Don't worry about it. Just be confident that if you are meant to take this step, then both the right Master and the money to pay their fee will appear.

The actual attunements are not very different from those that you will already have taken, the main difference being that you will be given the final sacred symbol, the Master symbol, Dai-Ko-Mio.

This symbol should be used to seal all your healing sessions; self-healing, Distant Healing and hands-on. Once learned, you will never forget it. Dai-Ko-Mio adds a power to your healing that you did not even realise was lacking before. You will swiftly become aware of a new dimension in the vibrations between you and the patients you treat.

This fourth symbol "crowns" the three symbols you have previously received. Use them wisely. You are now a Reiki Master.

Below: you will swiftly become aware of a new dimension in the vibrations between you and the patients you treat.

TEACHING REIKI TO OTHERS

In becoming a Master, you have accepted the responsibility of teaching Reiki to other people. This task is in addition to your normal healing work. Indeed, you may well find that as you pass on your knowledge to your students, your own healing powers will noticeably increase.

Below: in becoming a Reiki Master you must feel an overwhelming conviction that it is your task to pass on to other people the benefits you yourself have gained.

Your own Master will have ensured, to the best of their ability, that you are capable of fulfilling this extra responsibility. They will have asked you about the treatments that you have been giving and seek assurance that you have been having some success.

But the bottom line is that you yourself are the best judge of whether you are ready to pass on your knowledge to others. There can be no two ways about this. You cannot undertake this work half-heartedly, tongue in cheek, or simply to achieve a certain status.

There can be only one reason for undertaking the work of a Reiki Master. You must feel an overwhelming conviction that it is your task to pass on to other people the benefits you yourself have gained.

Don't be influenced by the suggestion that "Reiki is the in thing and I can make a lot of money at it". If this is your attitude, we can almost guarantee that you will fail in your undertaking. It is true that Dr Usui himself claimed that services given without payment are not valued.

Even so, your primary object must always be the good of your patients and your students. This means, simply, that you will charge a reasonable sum for your services, but that you will never ever turn away anyone who is unable to pay. Many Reiki Masters are so much convinced that this is the right attitude that they will not even advertise their services. They are confident that anyone needing their attention will find them and believe that to advertise would be to degrade their status and demean themselves.

If, after you have become a Master, you are asked to undertake the training of another person, you are honour bound to consider the pros and cons carefully. First – do not allow yourself to be influenced by any monetary incentive the would-be student is offering.

Below: "Reiki is the in thing and I can make a lot of money at it." If this is your attitude, we can almost guarantee that you will fail in your undertaking.

Right: ensure that you meet your would-be trainee on several occasions so that you get to know them well.

Second – ascertain exactly why they want to be initiated into Reiki. It is essential that those reasons are the right ones. Ensure that you meet your would-be trainee on several occasions so that you get to know them well. Discuss Reiki with them as much as is relevant to their present needs. Only when you are confident that this person has the right attitude towards Reiki training should you accept them as a pupil.

This is not the appropriate place to offer details of Reiki initiations. Indeed, as you have yourself experienced these initiations up to Master level, you will not need further instruction on the subject. Having become a Reiki Master, you will understand what is physically involved. You will also be aware of the mental and emotional state you should have attained before you are ready to give initiations. Suffice it to say that there is more to giving initiations than learning hand positions and symbols.

Y ou will obviously feel a little apprehension about treating your first
patient but, if you have made adequate preparations for this experience,
all should go well.

Below: some practitioners burn incense or a scented candle.

The section headed NOW YOU'RE A REIKI CHANNEL offers advice on how to prepare for a healing session. Obviously, the surroundings, your own clothing and your treatment couch must be spotlessly clean. Ensure that the lighting in the consulting room is comfortably subdued. You may like to play soft and gentle music. Some practitioners burn incense or a scented candle. You will gradually develop your own methods. What matters most is that both you and your patient should be totally relaxed.

When your client arrives, spend a few minutes chatting quietly with them, answering any questions they may have. Ask them to remove their shoes and outer garments. Then invite them to lie on their back on your treatment couch, hands at their sides. Encourage them to breathe quietly and regularly.

1 Sit behind your subject and relax, mentally as well as physically. With one hand draw the Power Symbol in the air above your subject's head. Patients can be tense and nervous at a first Reiki session. Rest your hands gently on their shoulders for a minute or two, just to let them know where you are and what you are doing. This will reassure them before you begin to move your hands around their body.

Now move your hands so that they are a few centimetres above your subject's forehead. Your palms should be facing down, fingers together. The thumbs should be close to the hands, and touching each other.

Maintaining this position, gently lower your hands until the heels of your hands are resting on the patient's forehead. Your palms should be covering their eyes and your fingers resting on their cheeks. Hold this position for about three minutes. Be careful not to lean over your subject and not to apply any pressure. At this stage, you should feel the energy flowing freely and later your subject may confirm that they shared the experience.

3 You may have difficulty in learning Position 3. For this reason, we advise you to discuss it with your Master and to practise with them until you are able to make the movements smoothly.

2 Gently separate your hands and move them over the subject's temples and ears. The change from one position to the next should be a smoothly flowing movement that does not disturb them. Again, hold this position for about three minutes.

Place your left hand under the left hand side of your subject's head. Use your right hand to roll their head over so that it is supported by your left hand. Then move your right hand under the right hand side of their head. Your subject's head should now be resting on both your hands, with your fingers touching and thumbs close to the fingers. If you are in the correct position, your forefingers should be able to feel a slight depression at the base of your subject's skull. Very gently press your forefingers up into this depression. Hold that position for the usual three minutes, gently cradling your subject's head in your hands. Most patients find this position exceptionally relaxing and comforting.

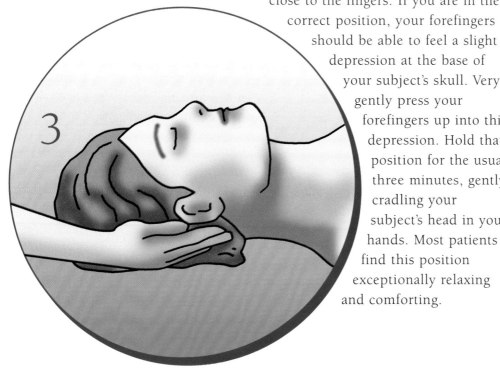

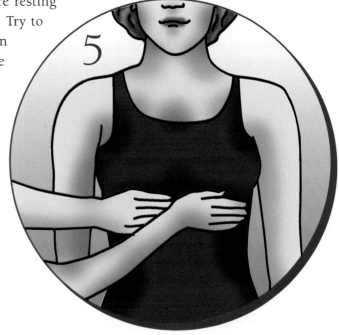

5 Stand up and move to one side of your subject. Try to do this without moving your hands from the subject's body. Most patients are reassured if hand contact is maintained throughout the treatment. With practice, you will soon find that this comes naturally as you work through the healing session.

Now place one of your hands on either side of the patient's body, at the lower end of the rib cage. Because you are standing to one side of the couch, this means that your hands will be in line, one behind the other. Try to ensure that the forefinger of one hand is just touching the wrist of the other.

4 Free your hands by gently rolling the patient's head first to one side and then to the other. Now slide your hands down so that they are resting on the patient's collarbone. Try to avoid resting your hands on their throat, as most people find this uncomfortable.

7 Slide your hands down so that you have one resting on each of the patient's hipbones, level with the pubis. Be careful about the placing of your hands in this position, particularly if your patient is of the opposite sex. Keep your hands on the outside of the hips, as though cupping them and pulling them towards the centre of the body.

6 Next, move your hands down to the pelvic area, slightly below the level of the navel.

When you are new to giving Reiki treatments, you may find it tiring to hold these positions. If so, we suggest you alternate the way you use your hands. Suppose that in Position 5 your left hand were extended and your right hand were nearer to you. When taking up Position 6, slide the hands down and cross them over. Your left hand will then be closer to you and the right hand will be more extended.

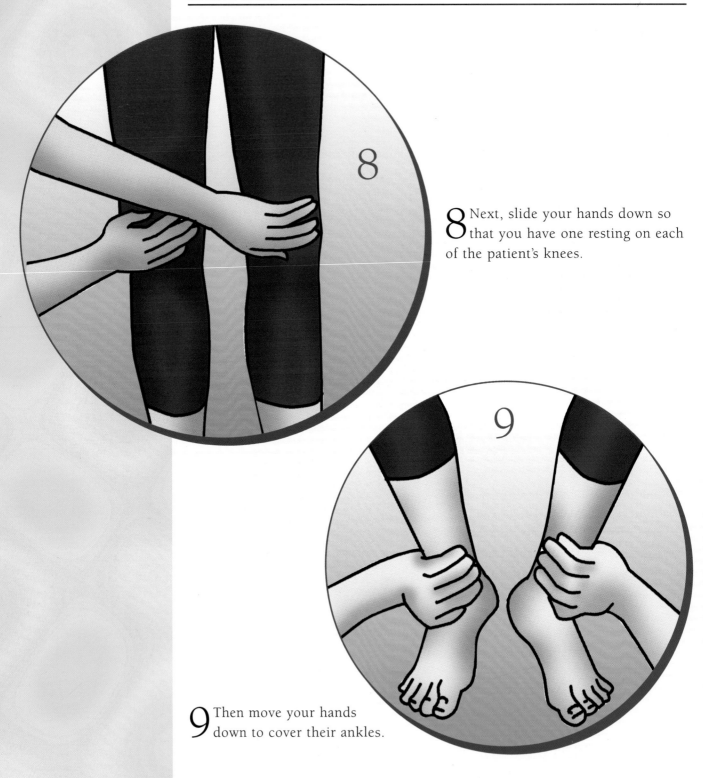

8 Next, slide your hands down so that you have one resting on each of the patient's knees.

9 Then move your hands down to cover their ankles.

10 Finally, to complete the treatment of the front of the body, move so that you can gently hold the subject's feet, one in each hand. Do this while you are standing at the end of the couch, so that you are able to hold each foot firmly.

This concludes the healing at the front of the body. Pause for a moment or two, then ask the subject to roll over on to their stomach. They will now be face down, their head turned to one side, arms bent and their hands positioned alongside

At this stage, remind your patient to maintain their quiet regular breathing. When they are again comfortable and relaxed, make the sign of the First Symbol above them. Then take their head gently in both your hands.

11 After this position has been held for three minutes, move your hands so that they are resting on their shoulders. This is best done when you are seated at the top of the couch.

12 Now move to the side of the treatment table, so that your hands are across the patient's back, level with their heart.

13 Slide your hands down to their waist. Remember to cross over the hand positions if you find this more comfortable.

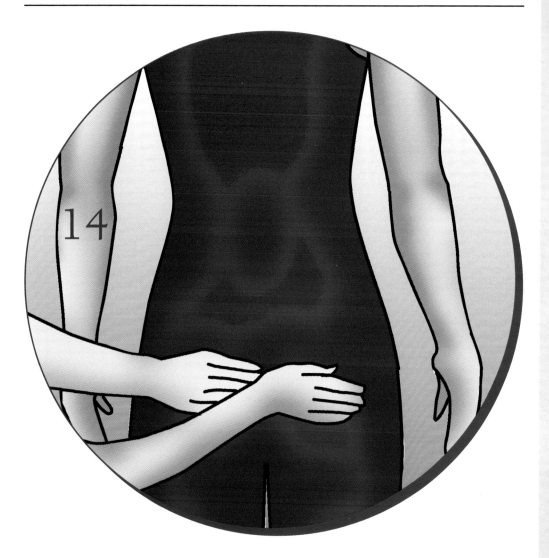

14 Next move your hands so that they are level with the buttocks. Again, remember to keep your hands on the outside of the hips.

15 As with Position 3, Positions 14 and 15 will need some practice until you can do them comfortably. The aim is to keep one hand at the top of the subject's thigh whilst sliding the other down to hold the foot of the same leg. Try this first on the leg that is nearer to you. Then reach over with both hands so as to take up the same position on the far leg.

16 Finally, rest one of your hands on each of your client's soles.

This finishes the hand positions and the treatment is almost ended.

THE END OF THE SESSION

Clear your patient's aura by moving your hands over their body, head to foot, about eight inches above the torso. Then draw the Master Symbol in the air above their whole body.

Quietly move away from the couch, but don't speak to your patient for a few minutes. Then touch them gently on the shoulder to indicate that the treatment is complete. Allow them time to compose themself, then ask them to sit up and rub their hands together. Offer them a glass of water and encourage them to take a drink. Finally ask them to step down from the couch and ground themself by rubbing the soles of their feet on the floor.

At this stage, most subjects are still "floating". Keep conversation to a minimum unless your patient is obviously anxious to talk. Then, just before they leave, ask if they want to make another appointment or if they would rather contact you later to do this. Be careful to maintain a quiet, relaxed atmosphere until the door closes behind your client. Then it is time to refresh yourself and the room in readiness for your next healing session.

The word "chakra" is a Sanskrit term meaning "wheel of light". It is used to describe the seven vibrating energy centres that exist within the body of every human being. These seven wheels are connected to a line of energy that runs parallel to the spinal cord. Each rotates at a different frequency and is identified by a number and a colour.

Below: illness is caused by an imbalance of energy or a lack of energy flow throughout the body system.

The chakras are invisible to the naked eye, though some psychics are able to see them. Each of these energy centres is about two inches or 50 millimetres in diameter. In the average person the energy of the chakras is shown by a dull glow, but in the more spiritually awakened the colour and light is intensified by the increased frequency of the vibrations.

THE IMPORTANCE OF ENERGY

The chakras may be thought of as the centres of spiritual power in the human body and are associated with the relationship between energy and matter. Their function is to provide a pathway for this energy to flow in and out of the aura.

Energy of a high frequency is transformed by the chakras into a glandular hormonal output that affects the physical body. Opening the chakras will increase the flow of energy and the more this flow is enhanced, the healthier the individual will be.

Illness is caused by an imbalance of energy or a lack of energy flow throughout the body system. This, in turn, can cause changes to the nervous system resulting in illness or dis-ease.

FINDING THE CHAKRAS

It is easy to locate the chakras within your own body. First, decide on which chakra you want to find. Sit quietly in a comfortable chair and close your eyes. The palms of your hands should be facing your body, about an inch away from the surface, and in the area of the chakra you are seeking (see chart below). Now wait patiently, confident that you will soon feel the vibrations of energy coming from that site. You may even "see" the energy as a softly coloured light between your body and the palms of your hands.

Don't be disappointed if your first attempt at this experiment is unsuccessful. Try again another day – but do remember that tension of any kind will nullify your efforts. It is essential that your mind and body should be completely relaxed.

NB: *Please note that we all have seven chakras, but the individual numbers and colours given here may be at variance with those quoted in other publications. This is not important. What matters is the* **location** *of each chakra and its effect upon your mental, emotional, spiritual and physical health.*

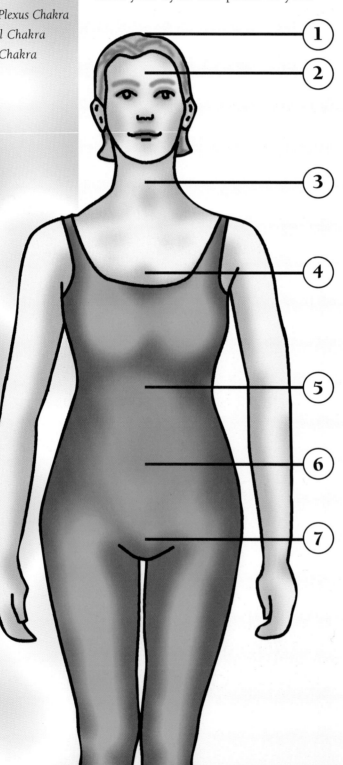

Each chakra is associated with a certain part of the body. Its job is to ensure that that particular organ receives the energy needed to function correctly. However, any blockage in the energy flow can also lead to problems on the mental, emotional and spiritual levels.

Generally speaking, the upper chakras (1 to 4) vibrate at a higher frequency and are associated with our mental, physical and intellectual functions. Those in the lower part of the body (chakras 5 to 7) are concerned with our more basic emotions and vibrate at a lower frequency.

1 THE CROWN CHAKRA

This, the first chakra, is located at the crown of the head (sometimes called the fontanel), and is associated with the pituitary gland. When this chakra is correctly balanced, you will enjoy good physical health. Balance here also promotes spiritual enlightenment and intuition.

2 THE BROW CHAKRA

Often known as the Third Eye, the second chakra is linked to the pineal gland and is found in the centre of the forehead, slightly above the eyebrows. This is the seat of ideas – a successful entrepreneur will almost certainly have a well-balanced brow chakra. However, if the vital balance is lacking, they may be too fearful to put his ideas into practice.

Left: when the crown chakra is correctly balanced, you will enjoy good physical health.

Below: the brow chakra is found in the centre of the forehead.

4 THE HEART CHAKRA

This chakra is found in the centre of the chest, in line with the heart, and is linked to the thymus gland. The fourth chakra is related to heart or lung conditions and with the circulation of the blood. Any imbalance in this chakra will result in feelings of depression and overwrought emotions.

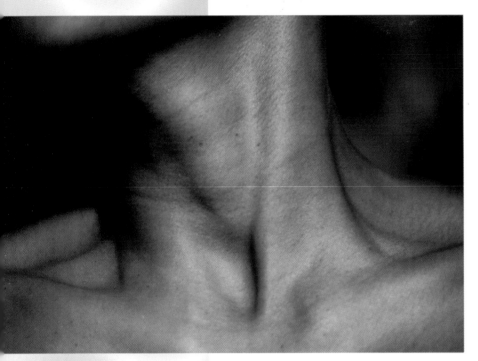

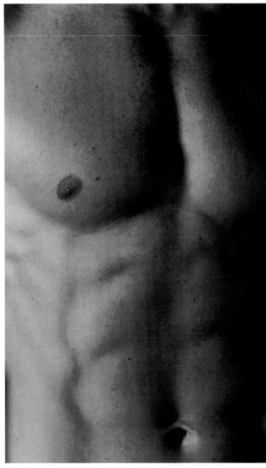

Above: the throat chakra is positioned in the throat and neck.

Right: the heart chakra is found in the centre of the chest.

3 THE THROAT CHAKRA

The third chakra, positioned in the throat and neck, is linked to the thyroid gland. For this reason, it affects the metabolism of the body and can become imbalanced as a result of stress and strain. When the throat chakra is functioning well, it can aid communication, self-expression and creativity.

5 THE SOLAR PLEXUS CHAKRA

The solar plexus chakra is to be found, at the base of the breastbone, and is linked to the pancreas. It is the seat of physical energy and affects the individual ego. Any imbalance here can be reflected in the emotions and will have a marked effect on personal relationships,

6 THE SACRAL CHAKRA

Sometimes known as the spleen chakra, this is positioned slightly above the navel in front of the sacrum. It is linked to the production of adrenalin. As a result it is associated with stress and how you deal with it. If this chakra is not functioning properly, you may experience physical problems in this area. A well-balanced sacral chakra enhances physical and mental energy.

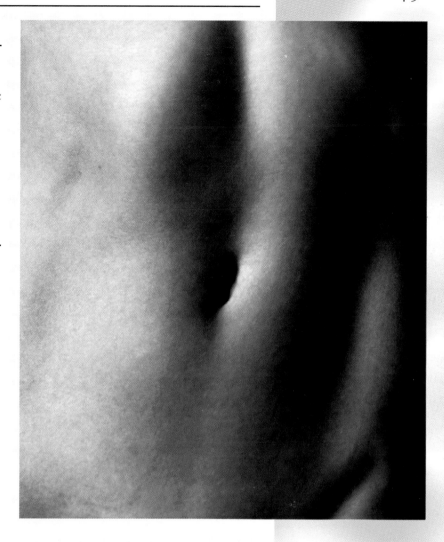

7 THE ROOT CHAKRA

Located slightly above the genitals, the root chakra is linked to the suprarenal glands. It relates to vitality, creativity and the urge for self-preservation. Imbalance can lead to mental instability, and excessive or unnatural sexual appetites.

Above: the sacral chakra is positioned slightly above the navel in front of the sacrum.

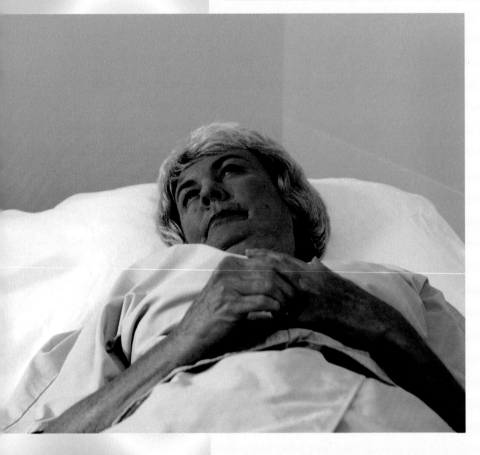

Above: you should devote a complete healing session to re-balancing the chakras if they are out of harmony.

REIKI AND THE CHAKRAS

If you are to enjoy complete mental, emotional, spiritual and physical health, the chakras must be perfectly harmonised. Should the flow of energy between these "wheels" be blocked or restricted in any way, Reiki can help to restore the vital balance.

Some forms of Reiki (Osho in particular) prefer to use the chakra positions rather than those taught by the Usui method. To avoid confusion, it is usually advisable to stick with one method or the other, particularly when you are beginning your Reiki practice.

BALANCING THE CHAKRAS

If you realise that one of your patients is particularly blocked, you will obviously need to address the problem. Our advice is that you should devote a complete healing session to re-balancing the chakras. Explain this to your client as clearly as you can. Make them comfortable on the treatment couch. Then simply place your hands on each chakra in turn for about three minutes. If your patient prefers not to be touched, it is just as effective to hold your hands slightly above their body.

The whole session will probably take less than half an hour, but you will need to allow time for your subject to adjust to the new vibrations they will be experiencing. Don't be tempted to proceed with the normal Reiki treatment immediately. It is far better for the patient to return a few days later when the chakras have settled to a regular vibratory pattern.

Primarily, Reiki is regarded as a healing tool. However, it can be used for other purposes, as has already been mentioned briefly. Before discussing such possibilities, though, we should emphasise that you must never try to use the power of Reiki in any harmful fashion. Remember, always, that in Reiki **intent is everything**. Ensure that you are seeking only what is good and beneficial for all concerned.

Many practitioners have changed lives – their own and other people's – by using the power of Reiki. This may sound airy-fairy and gullible. The fact remains that it is possible to use this power to change situations for the better, to achieve seemingly impossible goals, to conquer bad habits – even to "heal" your car or computer. There is no reason why Reiki should not be used to achieve material gains. The more you use the power, the stronger it becomes – but never forget that it is a force for **good**. Don't try to use Reiki maliciously. It won't work and you could be setting up a chain of unfortunate results.

Similarly, you should never use Reiki in an attempt to influence another person, unless you have discussed the project together. No matter how good your intentions, you must not try to "play God". We all have free will and this aspect must be respected.

Below: Reiki can even be used to "heal" your car or computer.

Above: the energy of Sei-He-Ki is particularly useful when dealing with any form of emotional or mental distress.

USING THE SYMBOLS

Each of the symbols has its own particular power and can be used in various ways.

Hon-Sha-Ze-Sho-Nen is the symbol used to send Reiki over a distance. Thus, it can usefully be employed if you are trying to resolve any situation outside the room in which you are standing.

The energy of **Sei-He-Ki** is particularly useful when dealing with any form of emotional or mental distress. It can resolve quarrels, mend broken hearts or help a worried student pass their exams. Use it, too, to cure bad habits like compulsive eating and nail biting, even addictions like alcoholism and drug abuse.

Cho-Ku-Rei, the Power Symbol, can strengthen the results obtained from using the other two symbols. Draw it on a piece of card and carry it in your car. It will protect you from accidents and delays and may even help you to find a parking space.

Whatever the problem you are trying to solve and whichever symbol you decide to use, the procedure is simple. Draw the symbol in the air and concentrate your thoughts on the desired results, just as you do when you are giving Reiki treatment to one of your patients

PUT IT IN WRITING

Another way of using Reiki to achieve your aims is to put your request in writing. Here again, methods vary.

Let us suppose that you have applied for a new job. Write your name on a piece of paper. Beneath it, write the name of the position you want. Add the Power Symbol – Cho Ku Rei. Sit quietly. Hold the paper between your palms and switch on to Reiki. Repeat this procedure for about 10 minutes every day.

It's a good idea, too, to carry the paper with you so that you see it frequently as you go about your business. Take time – perhaps as you drift off to sleep at night – to visualise receiving the letter offering you the job you want, at the salary you want. Be sure, though, that you are not requesting that another person should lose the job in order for you to have it. Reiki will not work that way.

Some practitioners even make a list of the various wishes they would like to have granted and then "process" the paper in the manner given above. You may use either method – or perhaps devise your own.

Below: one way of using Reiki to achieve your aims is to put your request in writing.

Right: "Be careful what you ask for. You may get it."

WHAT IS YOUR INTENT?

As we have said earlier, in Reiki intent is everything. Thus, you will appreciate that it is essential to give a good deal of thought to your requests before making them. You must never ask for something that will deprive another person. Remember, too, to carefully consider all aspects of the wishes you are voicing. There is an old adage that warns, "Be careful what you ask for. You may get it".

As a safeguard, it is always as well to make the proviso, "I ask for this or something better, if it is for my good and harms no other person."

WHICH SYMBOL TO USE

As a Reiki Master, you know the meanings of the symbols and the powers that they possess. It is not terribly important which one you use in this type of work. Remember that Reiki power always gravitates to where it is most needed. Concentrate on what you want and why you want it and leave Reiki to do the rest.

Don't be carried away with enthusiasm about this aspect of Reiki. It may take some time for your requests to manifest. In fact, they may not happen at all. In that case you can be sure that some other benefit will turn up eventually. Or perhaps you are unwittingly asking for something that is not rightfully yours. Consider, again, this aspect of your request.

Are you absolutely certain that what you ask for is right for you to have?

One final note of warning. Don't expect to use Reiki power to win the Lottery. Perhaps it is possible – but we've never heard of it. If you insist on trying, do let us know the result.

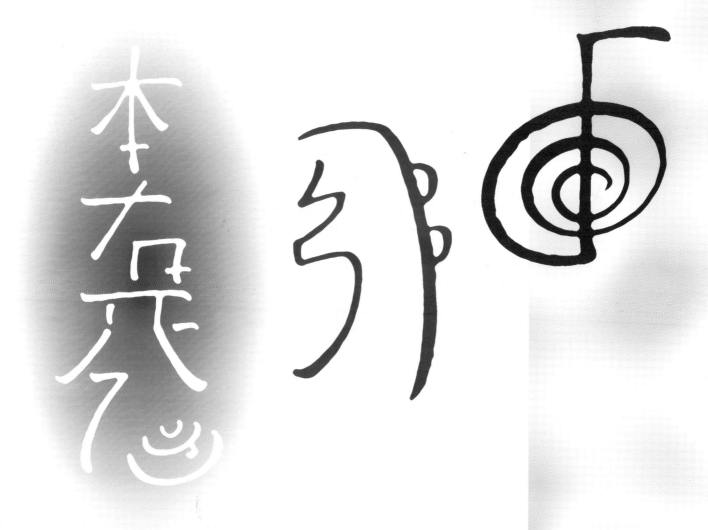

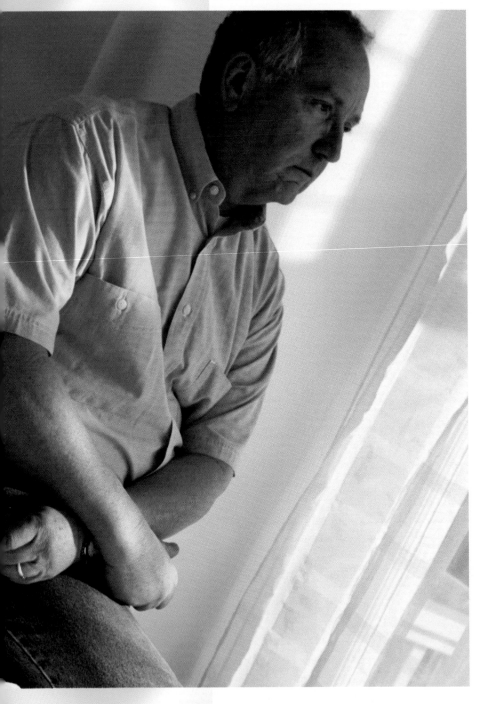

REIKI FOR THE OLD AND DYING

Even if elderly people are in reasonably good health, they are often lonely, short of money and generally depressed. Reiki can be of tremendous value in these circumstances. It will not necessarily solve their problems, but it will most certainly improve their mental and emotional state and enhance contentment in their twilight years.

Similarly, Reiki healing can be used to assist a peaceful passing for those who are beyond physical help. In this sort of situation, it is often enough for the practitioner merely to place theirs hands very gently on the sufferer. There is no need to use any particular hand position. Alternatively, the practitioner may simply stand in the room and use the symbol – Hon Sha Ze Sho Nen – for Distant Healing. Be assured that Reiki power can be only beneficial.

Above: even if elderly people are in reasonably good health, they are often lonely.

MISCELLANY

In these pages we have touched only briefly on the wide variety of ways in which Reiki power can be used. There are many more. Indeed, some Masters make a habit of giving Reiki to their food before they eat. Other uses include increasing the power of medicines, finding a soul mate, cleansing a room, or encouraging the growth of plants (especially if they are sick) – in short, Reiki can help you to achieve almost any goal you have in mind. We urge you to experiment in this direction. Devise your own mantras and rituals. Rest assured that nothing you do can be regarded as wrong or harmful provided you remember that **intent is everything**. We cannot over-emphasise the importance of this aspect. No matter when, why or where you use the power of Reiki, it must be in a positive fashion and to the benefit of all concerned. As long as you remember this one vital rule, Reiki will enhance your own life and benefit all those with whom you come into contact.

"When you heal yourself and assist others with their self-healing, you heal the Earth. You do make a difference."

Laurel Steinhice

Above: some Masters make a habit of giving Reiki to their food before they eat.

Left: Reiki encourages the growth of plants (especially if they are sick).

CASS'S STORY

We started on the path to Reiki a number of years ago, although at the time we didn't realise where we were going.

HOW IT BEGAN

Cass's problems started one morning when, on getting out of bed, he remarked, "I must have lain awkwardly. My back hurts."

Little did we realise, at that time, how swiftly and severely the pain would worsen. Within a month, it was so bad that he made an appointment to see an osteopath. Six visits did nothing but increase his suffering. Our GP prescribed pain killers. When they didn't help, he made an appointment for Cass to see a consultant – the first of several. There followed more prescriptions for pain killers. At one time he was taking 24 a day.

Below: the GP prescribed pain killers.

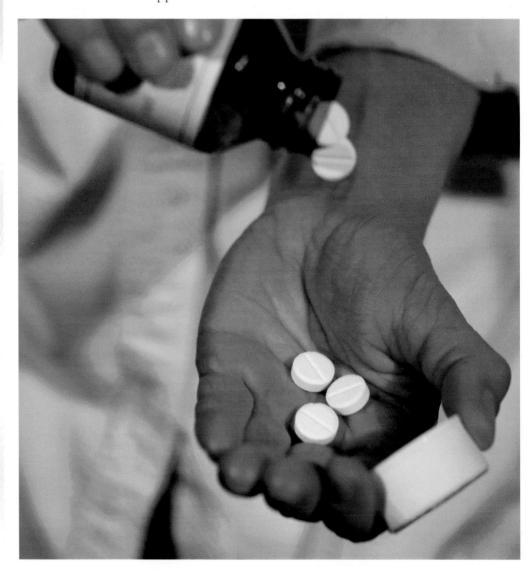

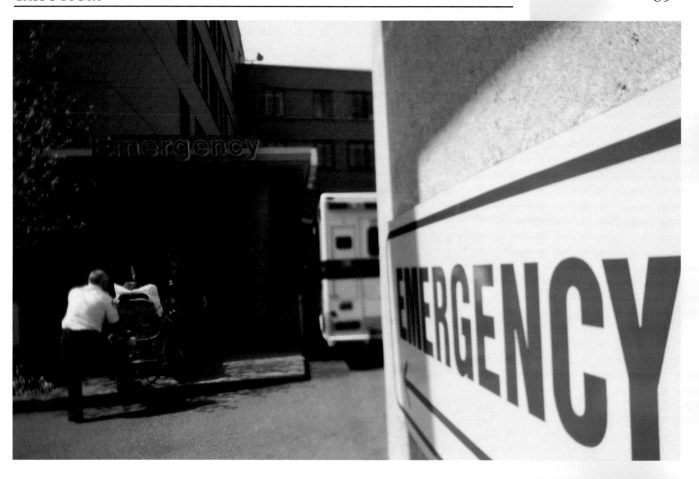

COMPLICATIONS

That in itself created more problems. By this time, Cass had been suffering agonies for two years. But there was worse to come. As a result of taking so much codeine, his elimination systems completely packed up and he was in even worse pain. A rush to A & E at the local hospital resulted in a two-hour wait for attention. When he finally saw a doctor, he was immediately admitted to hospital.

We will draw a veil over the next 12 hours. He returned home the next day, with strict instructions to avoid any tablets containing codeine.

With fewer pain killers, his back pain worsened. He was scanned and X-rayed, fitted with a corset, given an epidural and endured a spinal probe, none of which was in any way effective.

His pain increased. Even the short ride to the hospital for further investigation was almost too much for him. By this time, he was scarcely able to walk, and found it almost impossible to cope with stairs.

Above: a rush to A & E at the local hospital resulted in a two-hour wait for attention.

Moving house

That was when we decided we had to move to a ground-floor apartment. We decided, too, to move from the South Coast to Surrey, to be closer to most of our friends and family. There was also the faint hope that moving closer to London would get better treatment for Cass.

We moved in October, by which time Cass was in such a haze of drugs and torment that he cannot now remember this period.

Our new doctor was charming, prescribed more pain killers and suggested that she would make an appointment for Cass to attend a Pain Clinic. The first available appointment was six months ahead. By November his agony was beyond belief and he begged the doctor to "do something – anything – I can't take much more of this".

Right: in October, Cass was in such a haze of drugs and torment that he cannot now remember this period.

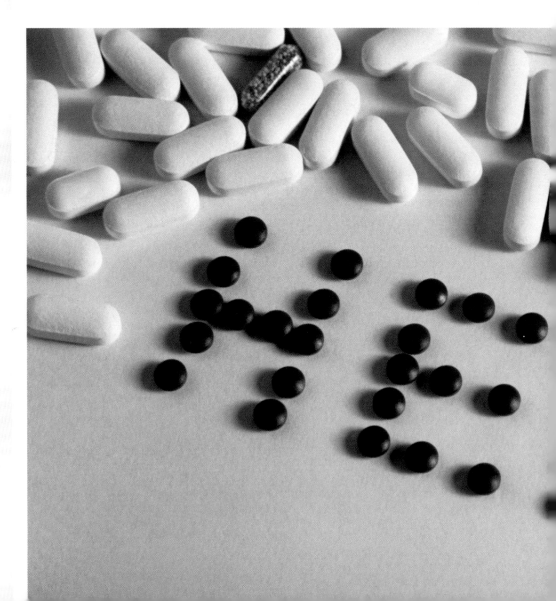

MORE DRUGS

Reluctantly, the doctor prescribed morphine. He took two doses – and began to vomit, which did nothing whatsoever to help the pain in his back. He had terrible head pains, was grey-faced and sweating. I thought he was dying – Cass just wished he could.

We called out the doctor. She said Cass was obviously allergic to morphine, so the only thing to do was wait until he could get to the Pain Clinic in April. Meanwhile, she gave him some Valium tablets.

One morning, when I reluctantly left Cass alone while I went shopping in the village, I saw in the Post Office window a small card giving the name of a local healer. But would Cass try it?

"I'll try anything," he said, desperately.

A phone call resulted in an appointment to see the healer, Peter, the next day. Somehow, Cass managed to get into the car. At the end of the 10-minutes drive he was sweating and shaking with pain.

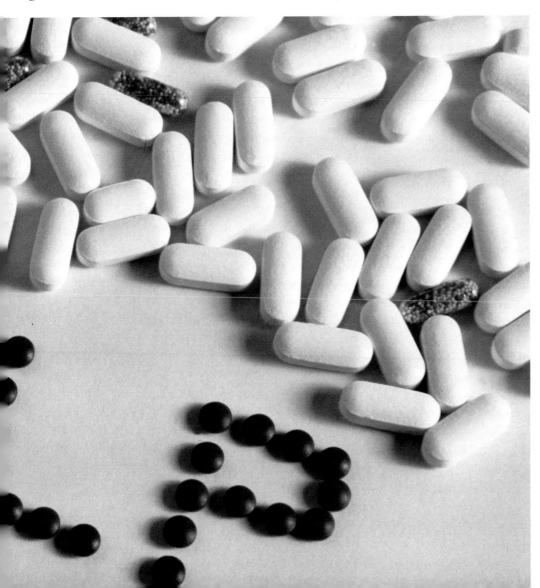

THE HEALER

Peter was a big, grey-haired, kindly man. "Let's see what we can do," he said. He helped Cass on to his treatment couch and asked him to try to relax. I watched as Peter began to place his hands in various positions on Cass's body. How was it possible that such simple actions could make any difference to the pain he had endured for so long?

The treatment lasted an hour. At the end, Cass was able to get off the couch unaided. What's more, he walked – albeit slowly and with a stick – to the car park 100 yards away. That was more than the sum total of the distance he had walked in the previous 18 months.

DISCOVERING REIKI

It wasn't until Cass had had half a dozen sessions with the healer that we learned the name of the method that Peter used. It was Reiki.

Cass received treatment once a week for six months. His condition improved noticeably after each visit. At the end of six months, he was free from pain and in better health than he had been for years.

That was when he decided to train as a Reiki practitioner and, in time, progressed to becoming a Reiki Master.

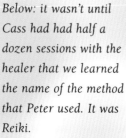

Below: it wasn't until Cass had had half a dozen sessions with the healer that we learned the name of the method that Peter used. It was Reiki.

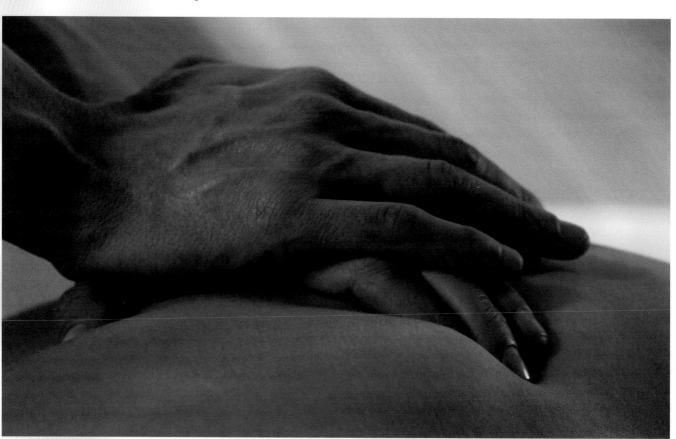

USEFUL ADDRESSES

BRITISH REIKI ASSOCIATION
2 Manor Cottages
Stockley Hill
Peterchurch
Hereford HR2 0SS
Send s.a.e. for a list of Reiki
practitioners in your area.

THE INTERNATIONAL CENTER FOR
REIKI TRAINING
21421 Hilltop #28
Southfield
Michigan 48034
USA

Courses, workshops and retreats
For information send s.a.e. to:
Penelope Quest
C/o Libra
8 Market Street
Kirkby Lonsdale
Cumbria LA6 2AU
E-mail: pennyquest@yahoo.com

FURTHER READING

HEALING REIKI
by Eleanor McKenzie
ISBN: 0 600 59258 5
Published by Hamlyn

REIKI FOR THE SOUL
by Mari Hall
ISBN: 0 7225 3891 X
Published by Thorsons

EMPOWER YOUR LIFE WITH REIKI
by Richard Ellis
ISBN: 0 3407 6628 X
Published by Hodder and Stoughton

REIKI
by Penelope Quest
ISBN: 0 7499 1935 3
Published by Judy Piatkus
(Publishers) Ltd

INDEX